WORSHIPING IN THE ZONE

How To Be Better At Worship

WORSHIPING IN THE ZONE

How To Be Better At Worship

Volume 1

Chip Vickio

First Edition

Contents

PREFACE

Can you describe what it is to worship God? I have found that the definition of worship varies from one individual to another, and people sometimes struggle to define it. The most popular concept of worship that exists today is that worship is a lifestyle – it's simply living a Godly life.

I propose something much different than that – different than the philosophy most of the worship books of today teach. My view is that defining worship as a lifestyle is a diluted definition – that worship is not a lifestyle, but a more focused, deliberate, reverent moment.

How did today's concept of worship get so watered-down? What really is worship? And how can we be better at it? These are questions that I hope to answer in this book.

"God is Spirit, and those who worship Him must worship in spirit and truth." (John 4:24)

INTRODUCTION

One of the greatest hitters who ever played professional baseball, Ted Williams, once said that when he was at bat and "in the zone", it was like the baseball had stopped over home plate, just hovering there, waiting for him to swing at it. Being "in the zone" was the moment he was so totally focused on the task at hand, it was like he was in suspended animation. At that instance, all outside distractions were eliminated and his mind and body were harmonized in maximum intensity and efficiency. When he was "in the zone", odds are he would not only hit the ball, put place it where he wanted it to go.

Many athletes experience moments when they are "in the zone". For example, a professional golfer who is playing at the top of his game often is "in the zone" when teeing off and swinging the club, letting his inner self take over in sort of an elevated state of consciousness. When he is in the act of hitting that ball, he is so focused, the television cameras disappear, the spectators vanish, and the only thing he is concentrating on is putting the ball in the hole.

The same scenario is true for basketball players. I sometimes wonder how they can shoot a foul shot successfully while the opposing crowd is waving their hands and yelling in the background. The people in the stands do their best in trying to distract the player. However, they are rarely thrown off by the crowd if they are "in the zone". When this happens, all distractions are blocked out, the crowd disappears and it's only the player, the ball and the basket.

Musicians sometimes use the term "in the groove" as sort of being "in the zone" musically. It's the point when they are playing an instrument and find themselves flawlessly executing a song, in tune with their emotions and abilities, effectively expressing themselves through their instrument. At that point, they are sort of caught up in the music. The presence of the audience fades away and they are in perfect harmony with their instrument.

Being "in the zone" is a time of complete focus. Why shouldn't that be true of our worship of God? It's a perfect condition for real, meaningful worship. Does He deserve any less? I say when we worship, let that moment be a time when we are "in the zone" with God!

CHAPTER I

MY FORMATIVE YEARS

Years ago, I didn't pay much attention to the concept of worship. I was a believer in Christ since a child, but I wasn't really living as a devoted Christ follower. And I certainly wouldn't have considered myself as a worshiper unless it meant just attending church once in a while. I guess that's what I thought worship was – attending a church service. I would later come to realize that worship is much more than that.

I was a Rock & Roll drummer for most of my teen and college years, playing in various bands – mostly regional. I loved bands and loved music, and still do.

I started in music at a very young age. My first venture into the realm of music was a toy drum at the age of about six or seven. When I was about eight, my grandparents and parents were convinced that I would love to play the accordion. I believe that was mainly due to the fact that they were of Italian descent, and they missed the old Italian songs.

So, sure enough, they purchased an accordion, which by the way, was bigger that I was, and I began taking accordion lessons. It was the first and only time that I ever took music lessons in my life. From then on, as I progressed over the years to drums, piano, guitar, bass, mandolin, sax, marimbas, and harmonicas, I only played by ear.

I never really had a passion for the accordion, but I did well, and it did give me a foundation of music theory. And, yes, I do still have the accordion.

As a teenager, my real passion was the drums. I remember my cousin, Johnny, who was my age, had borrowed a drum set and set it up in his basement. We were probably around 14 or 15. It was an old set with a snare, bass drum, hi-hat, a couple of tom-toms, and a cymbal. The floor tom was so old that it had calf skin heads.

I can still feel the excitement I had when I first saw that set. It was the first time I saw a complete drum set in real life and I was fascinated. I don't know what happened, but this feeling I can't quite describe came over me – it was like an affinity or spontaneous attraction that drew me to them. It was love at first sight. I knew I had to learn to play them.

So I started. We took turns playing that set. Then, as young teenagers, we decided that we had to start a band. Johnny wanted to play electric guitar, and knew some other musicians, but they needed a drummer, so guess what – I volunteered. And off went my so called career as a musician.

We had to come up with a name, so we chose "The Cyclones". Our first job was at a high school dance. The school paid the band a whopping $25. I'm sure we were terrible. But we sure had fun.

We grew and developed as musicians from that point on, and got better and better. The bands changed and the musicians changed, and over those early years, my passion for playing music grew and grew. "The Cyclones" transformed into the "Mad Addicts." What a name! I laugh at it now. We didn't even know about drugs or addiction at the time.

By my college years, I was playing drums five nights a week in a house band at a nightclub, playing rock and roll covers. By that time, different musicians came and went, and we were known as "Jacob's Ladder."

After college, still playing music with my cousin Johnny, who by then was playing a Hammond B3, the band "Bo Jake" was formed. It became a popular regional band in upstate New York. We were based in Watkins Glen.

It was in this band that my songwriting foundation began. "Bo Jake" was a rock band playing mostly original songs. We did some studio work and played in the region.

During this time I toyed with songwriting on acoustic guitar. This would help me in later years with songwriting skills.

"Bo Jake" lasted a few years, things changed, and I went through various other bands as a drummer, traveling up and down the east coast, from Florida to Connecticut playing music.

I played drums in top 40 bands, rock bands, and jazz bands. In later years I played acoustic guitar and sang as a soloist, but also in duos, and small acoustic bands playing everything from pop to country to blue grass.

And boy, do I have the stories from all these experiences, but that's for another book. The reason I'm explaining all my background is to show that all along, God was preparing and equipping me to be where I am now, using my talents for His glory, leading others to be worshipers.

I must admit, in those early years, I didn't dwell much on the term worship, and honestly, I didn't practice it at all. It was only in my thirties that my real spiritual journey began. I had no prior knowledge of the Bible, but jumped into it with all I had. And my passion for playing music never ceased during that spiritual transition.

My wife and I joined a small church, and I slowly began using my musical skills for the Lord. Over the years, as the church grew and grew, I went from occasional back up musician to full time worship leader in charge of praise teams, lights, sound, and video. And ultimately I became in charge of the entire Sunday morning service, except for the sermon of course.

[See *Appendix B: My Personal Journey*, in the back section of this book, for a detailed account of how I went from volunteer song leader to full time Worship Leader.]

CHAPTER 2

THE CHALLENGE

When I first became a full time Worship Leader, my preacher challenged me to study worship for a year. What turned out to be a one-year project, turned into what seems to be an ongoing challenge. It started out when my preacher gave me a book on the subject of worship. What I didn't realize at the time was the fact that there were tons of books on worship. As soon as I would read one, he would hand me another. I had worship books in my living room. I had worship books in my bedroom. I had worship books in my bathroom, in the car, and in the office. After a while, I had stacks and stacks of worship books.

You know what I found out? Most of these worship books seemed to emphasize one thing in common – that worship was defined by how you live your life. The more I began to read, the more I realized how many authors equate worship to Christian lifestyle.

Some authors say simply listening to a sermon is worship. Others say that any action we do that glorifies God is worship. I've read that teaching someone about Jesus is worship, serving others is worship, preaching is worship, obedience is worship, giving money in the Sunday offering is worship, and giving our life for God's use is worship. Obviously, all these are good and honor God, but are they really worship?

The more I thought about it, the more it seemed to me that there must be something more specific about the practice of worship than just living your life for God. I began to question the common definition of worship

11

taught and accepted in our culture today. So, I suppose you could say, that's when my real search started.

I began with a search of the Internet for the meaning of worship. That was a mistake. The Internet will give you even broader results, some of them outrageously wrong. Here's a warning. If you go online to try to define worship, you will come up with every philosophical variation possible, and come away even more confused than when you started.

This idea of defining worship as a lifestyle really bothered me. Using that philosophy, someone could technically be worshiping God without even realizing it! That's crazy. How can real, personal worship happen without even being aware you're doing it! Something is wrong with this picture!

I wanted to get to the essence of worship. Our God is worthy of our personal, intentional, meaningful, heart-felt worship. But it seems like so many only understand a watered-down concept of worship. Not surprisingly, it seems to go along with the trend in other areas of our society today – to water down what were once conservative views into more liberal, tolerant philosophies. Just look at the moral standards of today versus fifty years ago.

Many times even our biblical teaching and practices have become compromised. Could this be true of our worship also? Is it possible that we have watered-down our worship so much that we are taking what should be a concentrated, focused effort and turning it into a thinned out and diluted concept?

Serving God, living for Him, evangelizing, singing, witnessing, and being a Christian example to others all seem to be grouped together to bring a broad definition of worship for many people today. But is this generalization of worship really what the Lord desires? Are the changes in our culture driving change regarding our philosophy of worship? Should it?

I once attended a Worship Leader seminar in Austin, Texas. The event offered several workshops on all kinds of subjects pertaining to leading worship. There was one on the schedule that caught my eye, so I registered for that one. The topic was worship theology. I was really curious on how the instructor would define worship. Sure enough, he offered a definition of worship that was incredibly diluted. He said, "Worship is everything we do in life that is pleasing to God". I thought to myself, "You've got to be kidding! Everything we do in life that is pleasing to God is worship?" During the seminar, he even used the illustration of a husband serving his wife by doing the dishes, and called that an act of worship. What?! Doing the dishes for your wife is an admirable thing to do, but is that really worshiping God?

There are a lot of things we do in life that are pleasing to God, yet we may not have God in mind at all at the time. This idea of worshiping God without even acknowledging Him is wrong.

Yet, there are so many in influential roles who promote this concept, that worship is everything we do in life that is pleasing to God. Let me tell you, that is not true worship. That is not the worship that the Lord desires. Yet, this watered-down philosophy is more accepted than ever.

At a concert I attended, the lead singer of a popular Contemporary Christian band exclaimed between songs, "Worship is our whole life!"

The problem is this – if we define worship in broad terms, that the way we worship is simply living

13

righteously, then our focus tends to be on us – on our life, our activities, and our service, and not on God.

Worship should not be based on a works philosophy. You see, worship should have nothing to do with ourselves. Worship is all about God, and nothing about us.

If I were to ask the question, "When did you last worship God?", what would your answer be? If you think that worship is simply fulfilling the duty of showing up on Sunday mornings and being present for the count, you are mistaken. Worship is not fulfilling a religious obligation, but involves a personal encounter with God. It's possible that one could show up to a Sunday morning worship service and never actually worship at all!

One of the consequences of many long standing denominational churches is the build up of man made traditions and teachings which have developed into rituals. As a boy in a denominational church, I remember being taught that if I were to fulfill all my obligations or rules of the church, such as never missing a Sunday service, observing all the designated holy days, and following all the customs and requirements of the church, then everything was fine between me and God. There was no teaching that I recall of a personal relationship with Jesus. There was no real emphasis on knowing Him and worshiping Him on an intimate level. That's where the problem lies.

Religious teachings that are filled with man made rules and regulations instead of the truths of the Bible will ultimately result in an erroneous view of worship. Worship is not simply attending church, or living by all the rules. God seeks those who will worship Him in spirit and in truth, not in fulfilling obligations and rituals.

Without a clear understanding of worship, we tend to make worship whatever we want it to be. When the

Israelites had no king, the scriptures tell us that everyone did what was right in their own minds. That was not a good thing, and it still is not a good thing. The problem with everyone doing what they think is right usually results in endless opinions and arguments.

Is it possible that most people don't really know how to worship God because they simply do not know what worship is? Could everyone be worshiping according to what is right in their own mind and not what is right in God's mind? If worship can be everything and anything we do, then essentially worship ends up being nothing!

Chapter 3

SEARCHING FOR A WORSHIP DEFINITION

Early on, I was hoping to find a verse, one verse in the Bible, that simply gave a definition of worship. Unfortunately there is no scripture verse anywhere that gives a simple, one-sentence definition. There's no Bible verse that starts with the words, "Worship is..."

This is not true with many other biblical doctrines such as faith, which is defined with scripture.

"Now faith is the substance of things hoped for, the evidence of things not seen." (Hebrews 11:1)

Because worship is not defined in such a clear way, man has come up with many variations in its definition – some poor and some sound.

There's Old Testament worship, there's New Testament worship, there's false worship, there's idol worship, and so on. Some define worship very loosely and some define it very narrowly. How we worship depends on how we define it. If we can't define it properly, how can we worship properly?

Finding the definition of true Biblical worship is not any easy task. Just the word *worship*, however, reveals to us a lot. The dictionary definition of the word means to give worth, great honor, reverence, and respect to someone or something. When we think of worship, we think of adoration, extreme love and devotion.

To worship someone is to venerate someone – to lift them up above all things. It involves admiration beyond limit. The object of worship is elevated above all, is held in the highest regard, and is idolized and approached with awe and wonder. Man is captivated by the object of his worship.

That is why God is so against idol worship. He wants nothing to be held in higher esteem than Himself. He wants us to place nothing in our lives above Him. He wants us to hold Him in first place.

I decided to really jump back into the scriptures, looking to get a grasp how worship was presented in context, in its proper setting. This would surely give me a broad understanding of worship. That's when I decided to do a simple word search. My quest was to find everywhere in the Bible where the word *worship* or any variations of the word (*worshiping, worshiper, worshiped*, etc) was used, and read it in the context of the passage.

So I started out my search using the New International Version (NIV), and discovered that there were 254 places in the Bible where *worship* is used. I began to look up each one.

Then one day by chance, I tried another translation – the King James Version. What I found was both surprising and disheartening to me. Instead of listing 254, the King James Version used the word *worship* only 188 times!

I began looking at other English translations. I searched the New Living Translation for *worship* and found it was used 495 times! That's 307 more times than the King James Version!

This opened my eyes to realize that some versions of the Bible present a much different perspective of worship than other versions.

Prior to that first word search, I had never realized that one's concept of worship is directly dependent on which translation of the Bible is being used! A person's theology of worship can very well be contingent upon the opinions of the very men who were involved in writing a particular translation! This would be a lesson I would carry with me to this day.

For each version or translation of the Bible, it is up to the different translators to decide when and where to use the particular English word *worship* to express a particular original language Hebrew or Greek word.

It's obvious from the table on the next page that there is a vast difference between translators as far as choosing when to use the word *worship*. Notice how many times *worship* is used (including any derivative such as *worshiping, worshiped, worshiper, worships*). The numbers include both the Old and New Testaments combined.

Of Times "Worship" (including variations) Is Used:

Young's Literal Translation (1898) ....27 times

New American Standard (1995) ....181 times

King James Bible (1987)........................188 times

New King James Bible (1975) .... 197 times

New International Version (2011).......... 254 times

New English Standard (2016)..................295 times

New Living Translation (2015)............... 495 times

The Message (2002)............................. 544 times

Surely the liberal use of the word *worship* in many Bible translations has contributed to today's liberal concept of worship – that worship is simply a lifestyle – that we worship God with our whole life.

What in the world is a translation anyway? It's taking words or thoughts from one language and transferring them to another language, keeping the original meaning as close as possible.

My son is involved in Bible translation in Tanzania, Africa. He is part of a missionary team that translates Bibles into languages that have never had a Bible before.

I visited Tanzania and had the opportunity to see this in action. One of the translators on the team explained that there are sometimes challenges in finding a word in the target language that best matched the original Hebrew or Greek word that the Bible was originally written in.

She explained an instance where the English word *perfect* was used in a particular New Testament verse in our Bibles. However, in the target language, there was no such word for perfect. Obviously, they couldn't leave it out, so they had to come up with some word that gave a similar meaning or thought. The goal for their team is to most accurately keep the meaning of the original language. The translators decide what word to best use.

The other day a friend of mine said he was going to do a word search on the word *grace*. I asked, "Using which translation?" He had a look on his face like saying, "What difference does it make?" He hadn't given that any thought. I'm sure that's true with most people. After all, that's how I used to be. Early on, I had never even considered that the results of a word search can vary so much depending upon which Bible translation you use.

Chapter 4

WATERED-DOWN WORSHIP

In looking deeper into the issue of the many various versions of the English Bible available today, there are good points and bad points. Probably one of the biggest positives is that we have such accessibility to God's word. It's readily available, whether in book form, or online, or even on devices such as our phones.

Unfortunately, a real negative concerning the accessibility of so many Bible versions or translations is that, occasionally, the wording in a particular verse is so different between translations that it actually could convey a different meaning. Or a least cause confusion, at face value.

And believe me, there are many, many versions of the English language Bible available today. There are literal word for word Bibles which take the original Hebrew or Greek words and attempt to take them as directly as possible into English. There are somewhat looser types of translations such as thought for thought ones. And there are paraphrase Bibles that are basically Bibles in which the translators are putting the scriptures into their own words.

I prefer to stick with more of a literal translation when studying the Bible more deeply. Sure, thought for thought is easier reading and fine most of the time. And paraphrase Bibles are even easier to read, but they are sometimes too casual for me.

Let me demonstrate how the variations in Bible translations have caused conflicts and confusion in defining worship.

Virtually every Bible translation converts *shachah* (Old Testament Hebrew) and *proskuneo* (New Testament Greek), and their various forms, into the English word *worship*, and its various inflections. These Hebrew and Greek words mean a "bowing down".

However, in some translations of the Bible, the translators decided to also include the Hebrew *abhadh* (serve) and the Greek *latreuo* (serve), and their various forms, as root words for worship as well, perhaps influenced by the practice of Old Testament temple worship. The use of these additional words translated into the English word *worship* has been a factor contributing to a watered-down philosophy of worship.

In looking for verses that could cause confusion when comparing translations, I found one particular verse that is, in my opinion, probably the one that causes the most confusion in defining worship. It may be the greatest single contributing factor in promoting the philosophy of a watered-down definition of worship – that worship is a life style. It's Romans 12:1.

Let's look a little closer at this important verse. I've made a comparison of four of the many different available Bible translations of this verse. Notice that I've underlined the ending phrases for emphasis.

Romans 12:1 (Young's Literal Translation):

"I call upon you, therefore, brethren, through the compassions of God, to present your bodies a sacrifice - living, sanctified, acceptable to God - your intelligent service."

Romans 12:1 (New Living Translation):

"And so, dear brothers and sisters, I plead with you to give your bodies to God because of all he has done for you. Let them be a living and holy sacrifice—the kind he will find acceptable. This is truly the way to worship him."

Romans 12:1 (New King James Version):

"I beseech you therefore, brethren, by the mercies of God, that you present your bodies a living sacrifice, holy, acceptable to God, which is your reasonable service."

Romans 12:1 (Holman Christian Standard Bible):

"Therefore, brothers, by the mercies of God, I urge you to present your bodies as a living sacrifice, holy and pleasing to God; this is your spiritual worship."

So, is offering ourselves as a living sacrifice...

..."your *intelligent service*"?

..."*truly the way to worship him*"?

..."your *reasonable service*"? or

..."your *spiritual worship*"?

Can you see the confusion? Someone using the Young's Literal Translation would think that living a Christian life is an intelligent, logical way to serve and glorify God. That sounds reasonable to me. On the contrary, someone using the New Living Translation would think that living a Christian life is truly the way to worship Him, and even conclude that this verse is the Biblical definition of worship.

Someone using the New King James Version would simply think that living for God is the reasonable way to serve Him, while someone using the Holman Christian Standard Bible would conclude that living a life pleasing to God is spiritual worship. No wonder some people think that a husband doing the dishes for his wife is an act of worship!

So who's right? When you look at the original language, the last phrase of Romans 12:1, in Greek, uses the words "*ten logiken latreian hymon*", which literally mean "the logical service of you". Personally, I stand on those original, literal Greek words in this verse, which emphasize service, not worship.

I need to mention that the word *spiritual* in this verse, used by some translations, is unfounded in the original language.

The proper way of understanding the correct interpretation of this verse, as well as any verse, is to look at the context of the passage. So let's do just that.

Since Romans 12:1 begins with the word *therefore*, this verse is actually a response to the previous chapter. And when you look at Romans chapter 11, it's talking about the grace and mercy of God toward both Jews and Gentiles alike, offering to all, salvation through Jesus Christ.

How we respond to the truth of chapter 11 is what Romans 12 is all about. Romans chapter 12 is about how we are to live as Christ-followers. It's more than just giving our hearts to Him. It's how we are compelled by His grace, His mercy, His offer of salvation, and His love, to live for Him. It describes how we are to walk the walk!

Being a Christ-follower involves the sacrifice of our will, our time, and our actions, and being continually available to serve God however we can, living righteous lives, devoted to Him.

Our life, our service, certainly is spiritually motivated, sacrificial, and spiritually driven. However, is living such a life our "spiritual" worship? – the way to worship Him? Absolutely not! Here's why. If our daily Christian walk is equated with the way we worship God, you could essentially worship God without even knowing you're doing it. Crazy! Is that the type of worship God seeks? No!

How can you be spiritually worshiping God without God in the picture at all, without acknowledging His presence? It's sad that someone could live their life as one that is pleasing to God, and think that is the way they are worshiping Him. Here's a trustworthy statement: there's a difference between worship and service.

There's a difference between worship and service!

I think there are good translations of Romans 12:1, and there are bad translations, in respect to the intended original meaning of the verse. I've talked to those involved in Bible translation when I visited the translation team in Tanzania, and was questioning how they came up with the correct words for a new Bible translation. The answer they gave changed my whole perspective.

Their main concern was not whether a translation was a literal word for word one, or a loose thought for thought one, or a paraphrase one. Their concern was whether or not the translation was "faithful" to the original meaning of the verse.

I had never heard the term *faithful* before when applied to a translation, but it makes so much sense. A literal word for word translation can be not only be very difficult to read, but it can be virtually impossible to match every word with a corresponding one in a different language. A translation that's too loose can come across as an interpretation – a paraphrase – instead of a translation.

What's important is that each verse is faithful to the intended meaning of the original language that the Bible was written in. With that in mind, the faithful interpretation of Romans 12:1 is this: Because of the surrender and sacrifice of Jesus on the cross for our salvation, and God's mercy and grace towards us, it is only logical for us to respond by living holy, obedient lives that glorify God.

Some Bible translations capture this interpretation very well, and some completely miss the point and are misleading. The bottom line is this: Romans 12:1 is not the Biblical definition of worship. And it should not be the proof text in establishing the definition of worship as living a sacrificial life. Instead, Romans 12:1 should be looked at as the description of the type of life a worshiper should live.

Chapter 5

THE WORSHIP AND SERVE PRINCIPLE

Did you know that Jesus distinguished between worship and service? To me, this is a huge lesson. It's found in the book of Matthew, where Satan tried to get Jesus to worship him.

"Then Jesus said to him, 'Away with you, Satan! For it is written, "You shall worship the Lord your God, and Him only you shall serve."'" (Matthew 4:10)

This is an Old Testament quote, but it's said by Jesus, and therefore confirmed by Jesus as truth. Jesus used the word *worship* (based on a form of the Greek word *proskuneo*, which means to bow down). And He also used the word *serve* (based on a form of the Greek word *latreuo*, which means to serve or to do God's work). He separated the two.

It's no doubt that worship and service make up two very important parts of our spiritual walk. Both are essential. Both are fulfilling. Both are purposeful. Both are pleasing to God.

Service should be the natural extension of a worshiper's heart. Who we are internally drives what we do externally. Spiritual worship leads to outward service. Worshipers are compelled to serve God. But service is not worship, and that seems to be the common misnomer today.

Worshipers are compelled to serve God!

The idea that we must worship and we must serve goes way back – all the way back to the 10 commandments. The second commandment distinguishes between worship and service, but also implies that they both are important. I underlined for emphasis the section that refers to worship (bowing down) and service.

"You shall have no other gods before Me. You shall not make for yourself a carved image—any likeness of anything that is in heaven above, or that is in the earth beneath, or that is in the water under the earth; you <u>shall not bow down to them nor serve them</u>. For I, the Lord your God, am a jealous God, visiting the iniquity of the fathers upon the children to the third and fourth generations of those who hate Me" (Exodus 20:3-5)

There's a problem when one focuses so much on service alone that they leave out their personal worship of the Lord altogether, and see their service as their worship. Because of that, they never really experience the real, intimate worship of God! And it may simply be the fact that they don't really know what worship is in the first place.

Without a doubt, the distinction between worship and service can sometimes be a fine line. And there are times when they actually may blend together, but only if we are intentionally and consciously worshiping God on the inside, while at the same time we are serving Him on the outside. Then, and only then, can worship and service go on at the same time.

However, if we are not consciously aware of God's presence and we are not engaged with Him, then service is simply service. We can help others with good intentions and a good heart, and we should. But a good deed can simply be just that—a good deed. A good deed is a noble effort, patterned after something Jesus would do. A servant's heart is a noble thing for sure. But serving on its own merit cannot be defined as worship.

If there is a distinction between worship and service, then what is service? Let's define it by looking at who a servant is.

One who serves is one who is living as a servant, always humbly and willfully available at the master's every call. A servant is an obedient slave living under the master's care.

As a bond servant, one who serves God is ever obligated to live righteously and always ready and willing to do God's work. That doesn't mean they are constantly worshiping the master. We need to worship God and serve Him also. They are both important, but both different.

The servant always wants to please the master, and make the master look good. As Christians, we are servants who are always available to represent the Master and faithfully administer His grace in various forms.

A true worshiper has a submissive attitude, and wants to live for Christ and love Him with all his heart, soul, mind and strength. True Christians will surely become living sacrifices for Him, being available for whatever work advances the Kingdom, ministering to others and glorifying Him. Worshipers are servants!

True worshipers will be compelled to serve the Lord and be driven to live their lives for God. The force that compels is love. God's love drives worshipers to serve and minister – to take action.

"For the love of Christ compels us, because we judge thus: that if One died for all, then all died; and He died for all, that those who live should live no longer for themselves, but for Him who died for them and rose again." (2 Corinthians 5:14–15)

A true worshiper has the right perspective of Jesus and knows who He is. One who worships the Lord will naturally serve Him, and live for Him.

One who worships the Lord will naturally serve Him!

Chapter 6

THE THREE KEYS

If worship is not service, or living a Godly lifestyle, then what exactly is worship? How would you define it? For me, in my quest to understand worship, and ultimately practice it, I decided to look at all the Biblical examples I could find of people worshiping God. I felt that only then could I get a good foundation of what it is to worship the Lord.

Here's what I concluded. There are three conditions that seem to exist in every instance of true worship. Unless all three of these elements, or conditions, are in place, then real worship isn't happening.

In this next section, let's discover these three conditions that are the essential keys for real, authentic worship.

KEY #1: A SPIRITUAL ENCOUNTER

True worship involves a spiritual encounter with the Lord. It's when we are in the moment, connected with Him. Worship is a spiritual experience, just as prayer is a spiritual experience. How can we possibly worship God unless it is a spiritual experience? It is essential.

If our worship is not a spiritual encounter, then it is empty and void. It would be like saying that you could pray without it being a spiritual act. Unfortunately, if that's the way you pray, then it's not prayer at all. It's vain repetition, or meaningless prayer. In true prayer we connect spiritually with God. The same is true regarding worship.

We, as Christians, are able to come into a spiritual encounter with the Lord. And the more we come to know Him and understand who He is, the more we will want to communicate with Him and be in His presence.

Because worship is an intimate, spiritual encounter, it is relational. This relationship aspect is so important. Without it, we are back to a religious obligation – a "works" type of worship.

When we are in a loving relationship with the Lord, we desire to please Him, to honor Him, and to worship Him. In false, idol worship, there is no relationship. There is no encounter, and it is not spiritual. When Jews wrongly worshiped the golden calf while Moses was on the mountain, what kind of relationship was that? God is not some inanimate object – dead, lifeless, or non-responsive. God is alive, and in true worship, we come into His presence. And we encounter Him. And that's a powerful moment, indeed.

Jesus changed the mode of worship forever when He taught a great lesson about the spiritual aspect of worship. It's found in John chapter 4. In this chapter, Jesus meets the woman at the well, and they enter into a discussion.

"The woman said to Him, 'Sir, I perceive that You are a prophet. Our fathers worshiped on this mountain, and you Jews say that in Jerusalem is the place where one ought to worship.' Jesus said to her, 'Woman, believe Me, the hour is coming when you will neither on this mountain, nor in Jerusalem, worship the Father.'" (John 4:19-21)

Notice that the woman regards worship as restricted to a place. Jesus explains that worship is not connected to a physical location, but is a spiritual encounter.

"But the hour is coming, and now is, when the true worshipers will worship the Father in spirit and truth; for the Father is seeking such to worship Him. God is Spirit, and those who worship Him must worship in spirit and truth." (John 4:23-24)

Jesus teaches that worship is not service, or works, or rituals, or a place, or even laws. It is now to be done "in spirit and truth". We can't just glide over this lesson from Jesus. It's a very important one.

Jesus defines who "true worshipers" are. True worshipers are ones who worship the Father "in spirit and truth". God is spirit, and we must worship in spirit.

Worship is a state of the mind and heart, as well as the spirit.

The Old Testament temple has been replaced by the temple of our own souls. Christ lives in us! And we, as Christians, are the spiritual temple. If we are in Christ, then worship is a spiritual encounter, and our hearts and minds need to be engaged.

The words of Jesus are not just about the spirit though. He includes truth. We must worship in spirit and truth. What is He talking about?

There are many teachings on what "truth" means in the above verse, and I suppose there are more than one that could be correct. However, my take on this is two-fold.

First, our worship must be directed at the truth of who God is – who Jesus is. This requires faith. Without faith, believing in the one we are worshiping, what good is our worship? If we are not worshiping the one true God, then we are not worshiping in truth. It is therefore fake worship of a false god.

We were all created with the ability to worship. That's how God designed us. So in that regard, we have an innate sense to worship someone or something. That's true of every civilization that existed. Unless one knows God, other things that are attractive or majestic or have splendor will be worshiped.

Over the centuries, the worship of various gods and goddesses have been practiced. The Greek and Egyptian civilizations, among others, were known for this. Some religions worship objects of nature – the sun, moon, stars, animals, and even fire.

But we are believers, Christ-followers. And we worship the one true God, the Lord of lords, and the King of kings. Therefore, we worship in truth.

Secondly, regarding truth, this can additionally imply that our worship must be sincere and real. Our worship cannot be fake, or just going through the motions.

It's important to note that those who are worshiping in spirit and truth are the type of worshipers that the Father seeks. This means God is looking for true, spiritual worshipers.

If you consider worship as doing something that is not spiritual, that is not a spiritual encounter with God, coming into His presence, as a believer, then it is not true worship! Perhaps this is the litmus test, the proof, when trying to determine what is worship, and what is not. True worship involves a spiritual encounter with the Lord!

True worship involves a spiritual encounter with the Lord!

Sometimes one's spiritual encounter with the Lord is planned, sometimes it is entirely spontaneous. In other words, you can purposely enter into the zone of worship. Or something could prompt you to worship God, and immediately come into His presence.

An example of planned worship is when Abraham was about to sacrifice Isaac. He intentionally stopped in his journey in order to worship God. He took a time out specifically to worship. Take a look at the scripture below that describes this scene.

"So Abraham rose early in the morning and saddled his donkey, and took two of his young men with him, and Isaac his son; and he split the wood for the burnt offering, and arose and went to the place of which God

38

had told him. Then on the third day Abraham lifted his eyes and saw the place afar off. And Abraham said to his young men, 'Stay here with the donkey; the lad and I will go yonder and worship, and we will come back to you.'" (Genesis 22:3-5)

Sometimes I'll walk on the beach near where I live, with the intent purpose of taking a few moments to stop and worship the Lord. It's planned. I'll go down to the water's edge, look out over the waves to the horizon, and intentionally worship God, expressing my thanksgiving, praise, and love for Him.

On the other hand, sometimes worship is spontaneous. In such cases, worship results as an immediate reaction or response to what God has done. I love when this happens because it's usually a time when our worship is very intense and focused, and we truly are worshiping in the zone. And it can be very emotional.

We can find many examples of spontaneous worship in the Bible. One such example is when the women unexpectedly encountered the resurrected Jesus.

"So they went out quickly from the tomb with fear and great joy, and ran to bring His disciples word. And as they went to tell His disciples, behold, Jesus met them, saying, 'Rejoice!' So they came and held Him by the feet and worshiped Him.'" (Matthew 28:8-9)

Regardless of whether our worship is planned or is spontaneous, it is done with an awareness – an awareness that we are in God's presence. It is truly a spiritual encounter.

If we bow in worship, even for a moment, it's on purpose, it's deliberate, and it's willful. There's no way we can bow down and not be cognizant of it.

How can you worship God without even realizing it, without even worshiping on purpose? You can't. That's why defining worship as simply living your life for God, or as a righteous life style, or as service, is not true worship.

You cannot worship God without being aware you are doing it!

Since worship is a time when we are in the moment, in the zone, with God, it has a beginning and an end. Worship therefore begins when we personally enter into it, and ends when we personally conclude it.

Worship occurs in a specific, focused, purposeful moment. It happens for a reason, and for a particular time period. It is a time when we deliberately stop everything else, devoting our full attention to worshiping God. This may last a brief moment or for an extended time but regardless of how long our worship lasts, worship is something we do on purpose, it's special, and it's spiritual.

KEY #2: A HEARTFELT ATTITUDE

Not only does our worship need to be a spiritual encounter with the Lord, but our attitude in worship must be real and genuine. It must be heartfelt!

To help understand what the word heartfelt means, let's look at some synonyms: earnest, sincere, honest, deep, true. Conversely, here are some antonyms: apathetic, aloof, dishonest, false.

Our inner man, our spiritual self, worships. If we do not worship God with a true heart, then we worship in vain. Our worship then is meaningless and futile. Jesus rebuked those whose worship was not sincerely from their hearts.

"Hypocrites! Well did Isaiah prophesy about you, saying: 'These people draw near to Me with their mouth, And honor Me with their lips, But their heart is far from Me. And in vain they worship Me, Teaching as doctrines the commandments of men.'" (Matthew 15:7-9)

In God's eyes, a sincere heart is not simply desirable, it's essential. He's looking for our hearts, and He's looking for hearts that are drawn to Him.

"Let us draw near with a true heart in full assurance of faith, having our hearts sprinkled from an evil conscience and our bodies washed with pure water." (Hebrew 10:22)

The primary factor that motivates us to have an attitude of surrender in worship is not God's power, authority, or dominion, but His love. His love is perfect and draws us to Him.

I heard Kim Walker-Smith, a popular Christian singer, say: "If you are not passionate about your relationship with Jesus, if you are not passionate about worshiping Him, it's because you don't know yet how much He loves you."

I think her words capture very well the idea that there is an emotional, heartfelt aspect to meaningful worship. And it's motivated by His love for us. That's because we enter into a loving relationship with Him – a father/child type of relationship.

The more we come to intimately know God, the more we realize there is nothing or no one that compares with Him. And the closer our relationship grows with Him, the more we want to give Him our admiration, our love, our devotion, our awe, and our reverence. And the more we want to worship Him.

When it comes to a heartfelt attitude, certainly humility comes into play as well. A humble attitude is demonstrated in virtually every Bible worship scene.

There is one point that all Bible translations agree on – no matter what the translation. It's that any Hebrew or Greek words (the original languages of the Bible) that mean "a bowing down" are translated into the English word *worship*.

It's my opinion is that this concept of *bowing down* is one of the essential keys to understanding what true worship is. Bowing down demonstrates an attitude of reverence, humility, and an acknowledgment of authority, superiority, and eminence. If I bow before someone, it's a personal demonstration of who I am in relation to whom I'm bowing down to.

Even someone who has never read the Bible has probably heard about the Wise Men. They deliberately came to find and worship the new born king of the Jews. Look closely to what they did when they found Jesus – they bowed down.

"And when they had come into the house, they saw the young Child with Mary His mother, and fell down and worshiped Him. And when they had opened their treasures, they presented gifts to Him: gold, frankincense, and myrrh." **(Matthew 2:11)**

These Magi, or Wise Men, were supposedly considered kings, or at least highly respected figures. So in bowing down, they symbolically laid down their crowns, displaying humility and reverence. They were paying homage to the new born king.

It's really amazing when you think about it. They came hundreds of miles to bow down before a king they had never met. And the king was a child! Certainly this demonstrated their humility, and their acknowledgment of Jesus being one of royalty, deserving of honor.

This act of bowing down by the Magi is a picture of humble worship. They could have simply approached Jesus and offered their gifts. But before they did that, they bowed before Him.

There are so many more examples of bowing down in worship that can be found in the Bible. A simple, yet powerful one, is demonstrated by Moses when he was on the mountain before God, receiving the ten commandments.

"So Moses made haste and bowed his head toward the earth, and worshiped." (Exodus 34:8)

When we think of someone bowing down, we think of the physical action. Although a physical bowing down could be a physical expression of inward worship, what's important to realize is that true worship involves an inward, spiritual bowing down.

The physical orientation of one bowing down signifies that nothing is more important, more cherished, and more honored than the one being worshiped. Bowing is a personal admission of personal submission. It is a physical demonstration that the one falling down is inferior and the one being worshiped is superior. It is in a sense an official recognition of who is King and who is the obedient, loyal and loving slave or servant.

Satan knew this concept well when he tempted Jesus in the desert. He knew what it would symbolize. If Jesus had fallen at Satan's feet and worshiped him, then it would have elevated Satan higher than Jesus.

"And he said to Him, 'All these things I will give You if You will fall down and worship me.'" (Matthew 4:9)

If Jesus would have done that, he would have exalted Satan and put Himself in an inferior position. It would have been a proclamation of who was the superior one. It would have showed that Satan was above all things, including Jesus.

We, however, know who we bow to. We bow to the Lord as King. And when we truly worship Him, it's always done with an honest, heartfelt attitude of Him being superior to us, Him being honored, Him being exalted, and Him being number one above all.

KEY #3: A PERSONAL EXPRESSION

For many, the question is, who should my worship be addressed to – the Father, Jesus, or the Holy Spirit? As Christians, we believe they are one in the same. One of the foundational beliefs for Christians is that Jesus was God in the flesh. And now, in the days after Jesus ascended into heaven, the Holy Spirit is present with us.

So perhaps it's a matter of how you, as a Christian, desire to direct a particular worship statement, depending on the situation. For example, say you are thinking about the cross and it prompts you to worship Jesus for dying for you, then address Him. Or perhaps you look at a beautiful sunset and it prompts you to worship God the Father for being the great creator of all things. Then address Him. If you feel guidance from the Holy Spirit and it prompts you into a worship moment, address Him.

One of the great mysteries of God is His three-in-one existence. I believe our brains are not created to be like God's, so we are not capable of fully grasping or understanding the trinity concept. We must simply believe it in faith.

Personally, I don't get too hung up on deciding who to address when it comes to worship, or prayer for that matter. It all works itself out naturally. The more you pray and the more you worship, it just becomes automatic who to address your worship or your prayers to. For in the end, they are all one in the same anyway.

Regardless of who you are addressing, worship involves a personal expression of some kind. This expression can take many forms. It could be expressing yourself by saying something out loud. On the other hand, it could be not saying something at all, but simply thinking a silent prayer.

It's also possible that when we are in the worship zone, we say or pray nothing at all, but just humbly and silently bow in His presence for the moment. And in that sense, we are expressing our reverence and awe.

Our worship is internal, of the heart and mind, although sometimes that could be accompanied by an outward, physical action.

Sometimes our worship is very emotional, and can bring us to tears. This often happens when we come into His presence realizing the extent of His grace, mercy, compassion, and love.

Let's look at three personal expressions of worship: prayer, singing, and physical actions.

THE WORSHIP PRAYER

Perhaps the most powerful personal expression of worship is prayer. There are many types of prayer, but there's something very specific about worship prayers: they have nothing to do with you, but everything to do with God.

They are not prayers in which you ask for anything from God concerning you or anyone else. A worship prayer must be selfless. In other words, it is not about yourself in a sense of a need or want. The act of worship is always a one way street – from you to God.

Worship prayers have nothing to do with you,
but everything to do with God!

Worship prayers most commonly express thanksgiving, praise, adoration, or awe.

By thanksgiving, I mean expressing gratefulness to the Lord. There are so many things to be thankful for. And when we are in the zone with God, connected spiritually, and with a heartfelt attitude, we could fill our whole worship time with an on-going string of thank-you's.

And by praise, it's exalting God for who He is and what He is capable of doing, and telling Him about it face to face. Praise can be defined as boasting about God. And when this boasting is addressed to someone else, it's called praise. For example, "God is my loving, compassionate Father who cares for me." But when this same statement is addressed to God, "God You are my loving, compassionate Father who cares for me", it's when praise becomes worship. And a string of praise statements can be woven together to make up a worship prayer.

Adoration is expressing your deep love and devotion to God. A worship prayer expressing adoration could be something as simple as, "I love you, Lord." Or you could express multiple reasons why or how you love Him.

And regarding awe, a worship prayer could be expressing amazement of Him - His power, His majesty, His splendor, His compassion. To be in awe of God is to be wonderstruck - astonished at His greatness. An example of a worship prayer expressing awe would be something like, "Father, You are filled with all majesty, honor, glory, and power." You could add to it all the attributes of God that amaze you.

To summarize, worship prayers are composed of thanksgiving, praise, adoration, or awe. Or a blend of them.

SINGING

Singing can be a great expression of worship, especially when the lyrics of a song are addressed directly to God. I refer to these types of songs as worship songs.

Worship songs are similar to worship prayers in the sense that they are sung from the first person, directly addressing God. And if worship songs are sung with sincerity and conviction, they become a powerful melodic expression of worship. I call such songs melodic worship prayers.

An example of a worship song would be one of my own original songs. It has the words, "You will not abandon me." In this line, I'm personally addressing the Lord directly, proclaiming his faithfulness.

I believe God created music for His glory. And certainly songs, especially worship songs, can be one of the greatest catalysts to help us worship in the zone.

Not all songs are worship songs. Some I categorize as praise songs. These are songs that are not addressed directly to God. For example, another one of my songs uses the phrase, "Jesus is the light of the world". You certainly could worship the Lord during this song, but the lyrics are not as direct or intimate. The words are about God, not aimed at God.

The third type of song that I personally distinguish from the first two is what I call a spiritual song. These types of songs are not addressed to God, nor are they about God, but are about the church, edifying and encouraging brothers and sisters in the Lord. For example, another one of my songs has the lyrics, "I'm going to build my house on the Rock of Jesus".

All songs can be categorized as either worship songs, praise songs, or spiritual songs. Worship songs, however, certainly are the most easily converted into personal expressions of worship. They can directly convey our thanksgiving, praise, adoration, or awe towards God. However, if what we sing is not from our hearts and minds, or is done without focus and awareness, it is not worship, but it is just going through the motions.

When it comes to categorizing the three types of songs, think about it this way: worship songs are "to God", praise songs are "about God", and spiritual songs are "about us".

Regardless of the type of song, when it comes to singing, we need to mean what we sing, and understand what we are singing and why. I really like the principle that is found in this verse.

"What is the conclusion then? I will pray with the spirit, and I will also pray with the understanding. I will sing with the spirit, and I will also sing with the understanding." (1 Corinthians 14:15)

PHYSICAL ACTIONS

Our internal worship may also be manifested outwardly. Such physical expressions can vary widely and include bowing, kneeling, raising hands among other things. It could be lying prostrate on the floor or simply raising or bowing our heads. It could be closing our eyes or covering our faces.

What's most important is what's internal, not external. Any outward physical worship expressions are really just byproducts of what's going on inside the heart and mind.

Sometimes, we just can't help it! It's automatic in many cases. And sometimes we can't just keep it inside! After all, if our worship is done with a heartfelt attitude, then there has be to an emotional aspect to it.

There's nothing wrong with displaying emotion during worship particularly if it's a worship moment centered primarily on praise, when our worship is celebratory. I've seen all kinds of outward emotions expressed during worship: from clapping to dancing to smiling to crying.

Of all the physical expressions of worship, raising hands is perhaps the most common one. Our congregation is a non-denominational one. Because of that, we have members from all kinds of backgrounds and denominations. The result is that many are uncomfortable with raising hands, especially those who grew up in more conservative denominations.

I personally like the idea of raising hands in praise and worship. After all, the practice of raising hands is found in scripture as expressions of prayer, praise, and worship. Below are a few examples.

"And so it was, when Solomon had finished praying all this prayer and supplication to the Lord, that he arose from before the altar of the Lord, from kneeling on his knees with his hands spread up to heaven." (1 Kings 8:54)

"At the evening sacrifice I arose from my fasting; and having torn my garment and my robe, I fell on my knees and spread out my hands to the Lord my God." (Ezra 9:5)

"Lift up your hands in the sanctuary, And bless the Lord." (Psalm 134:2)

To summarize, real authentic worship has three keys or essential elements. First, worship is a spiritual encounter with God. Second, it's done with a heartfelt attitude. And third, it involves some type of personal expression.

And when we experience such a spiritual moment of worship, we are conscious of it. We are completely engaged, focused, and in the zone with God. In that moment of worship we come to Him with humble, grateful hearts, exalting Him and honoring Him.

Considering the three conditions or elements, I have come up with a one sentence definition of worship:

Worship is that deliberate moment when you spiritually come into God's presence with a heartfelt offering of thanksgiving, praise, adoration, or awe.

Chapter 7

HOW TO BE BETTER AT WORSHIP

We can always improve our worship no matter how long we have been Christ followers. Below are a just a few ideas on how we can do just that.

1. BE POISED FOR WORSHIP

If our worship is not planned, then it is prompted by something. We need to recognize the many prompts that we may encounter, and be ready to respond in worship.

Here are some examples of worship prompts: seeing one of your prayers answered, lyrics of a song that touch your heart, seeing God's hand work in your life or someone else's, something beautiful in nature like a beautiful sunset or a moonlit sky, an unexpected blessing, and so on.

What's important is that when you encounter a worship prompt, you respond in a moment of worship, regardless how brief it may be. The more you practice this, the more natural your response will be.

Such prompts can easily and quickly be the catalyst to compel you to be worshiping in the zone with the Lord, experiencing a spiritual encounter, with a heartfelt attitude, resulting in a personal expression of thanksgiving, praise, adoration, or awe.

Here's an example of being prompted into worship. I particularly recall when one of my children was born I had a moment of spontaneous worship. My wife delivered by

C-section, so I had been present in the operating room, dressed in hospital garb. After the birth, when I went into the dressing room to change back into my regular clothes, my reflection on what just happened prompted me to spontaneously worship the Lord. I suddenly broke down in that moment, alone, in the zone with the Lord, talking to Him, expressing my thanksgiving and praise, and feeling overwhelmingly blessed. It was totally unplanned, it was for just a few minutes, but it was powerful and emotional.

It's so easy to miss the opportunity to worship God. I'm sure you agree that there are many experiences in your life that should have prompted you into worship, but didn't. Either you forgot about God in those moments, or perhaps you just muttered a praise statement about God with no focus or heart.

The more you are in the habit of acknowledging worship prompts, the easier and more frequent they will trigger worship moments for you. And your worship doesn't need to last long to be real. Sometimes it can just be seconds long!

I know for me, when something prompts me to be in the zone, in worship, it's usually very brief but intensely meaningful and authentic. It's personal and relational.

I suppose everyone is different on how they are prompted to worship God. But the main thing is that you should be in the habit of recognizing and responding to worship prompts.

Worship prompts are not restricted just for the good times. Worship can happen in bad times as well. Just look at the examples in the book of Psalms where David is struggling so many times, and yet trusts God and praises Him for who He is and what He is able to do.

Worshiping God in bad times can be simply a matter of proclaiming His faithfulness and His love. Or thanking Him for being there with you and never leaving you.

David demonstrates a great example of worship in bad times. When he was king, and his son was dying, David pleaded with God for his child to live. He fasted and laid on the ground all night.

The elders of his house could not get him to get up, or even eat food. After seven days, the child died. In the scripture below, take a look at David's response.

"When David saw that his servants were whispering, David perceived that the child was dead. Therefore David said to his servants, 'Is the child dead?' And they said, 'He is dead.' So David arose from the ground, washed and anointed himself, and changed his clothes; and he went into the house of the Lord and worshiped. Then he went to his own house; and when he requested, they set food before him, and he ate." (2 Samuel 12:19-20)

David could have blamed God for allowing his son to die. But instead, his response is amazing, and reflects his faithfulness. David worships God, accepting that God is the one who is all sovereign and in control.

2. VISUALIZE THE SPIRITUAL REALM

When you worship God, try to visualize God or Jesus. Perhaps He is next to you or in front of you. Imagine that you are in the throne room of God and try to picture what that looks like. Being detailed is not necessary. Just realize that worship is spiritual in nature just as personal prayer is. And realize that there is a spiritual realm that is real.

We worship in the physical realm but we are also spiritual beings, and therefore we worship in the spiritual realm as well. It's hard to fully grasp how all that works or what that looks like, but worship is definitely a spiritual encounter with God.

A descriptive account of what the spiritual realm looks like is found in the book of Revelation. What amazing insight this book gives!

The entire book of Revelation is a visualization. Chapters four and five are especially powerful regarding worship because these chapters give a description of John's incredible glimpse into the throne room of heaven. It's an intense and passionate scene with many words of praise and worship being offered around the throne.

Because of the book of Revelation's symbolism, it is difficult to fully understand and grasp the magnitude of heaven's worship. But it at least gives us a sense of hope and anticipation of the type of spiritual worship we will someday experience in heaven.

As for now, remember that when you are worshiping in the zone, you could say part of you enters into the spiritual "dimension".

3. ROUTINELY ATTEND CORPORATE WORSHIP

Being ready to worship on Sunday mornings is sometimes very difficult in our society. Everyone is so busy and so distracted. I have seen many instances where a family rushes to get to the Sunday morning services, leaving the house in a hurry and arriving either just on time or a few minutes late. The stress of getting a family ready to leave on time, dealing with traffic, and battling demands of children leaves little focus for God. In an hour long service, it may take someone who is not prepared to worship time to settle down and focus. If that takes 15 minutes, that's 25% of the service!

It's up to each one of us to properly prepare our hearts and minds. Even though it's difficult, especially in a family setting, there are ways we can improve our preparation for our worship in the Sunday morning assembly.

For example, try getting up earlier in order to leave not just on time, but early. Try reading some scripture or praying and meditating for a few minutes before you leave the house. On the way to the church building, instead of listening to the news or talk radio, listen to Christian music.

No doubt, there is something special when believers are worshiping together. The Lord's presence can be felt, and His Spirit is moving. Corporate worship happens when many believers are individually, personally worshiping God, yet doing it together, at the same time. Corporate worship doesn't necessarily happen by the mere process of gathering together. It's all about the heart of each person.

What I like about a worship service is that it can be very inspiring. And inspiration and encouragement should be a big part of a worship service. There are so many worship prompts when believers are together.

4. MEMORIZE WORSHIP SCRIPTURES

One of the best ways to become better at expressing worship is to imitate worship phrases that are found in scripture. The Book of Psalms is a great place to find these types of verses. Find some that you can relate to and put them to memory. Incorporate them into your prayers. Frequently review them.

Look for scriptures that address God directly. These types of verses can be great models to use as intimate expressions to God. Below are a few examples of the many such scriptures found in the Bible.

"You are worthy, O Lord, To receive glory and honor and power; For You created all things, And by Your will they exist and were created." (Revelation 4:11)

"For Your mercy is great above the heavens, And Your truth reaches to the clouds." (Psalm 108:4)

"Yours, O Lord, is the greatness, The power and the glory, The victory and the majesty; For all that is in heaven and in earth is Yours; Yours is the kingdom, O Lord, And You are exalted as head over all." (1 Chronicles 29:11)

"Your word is a lamp to my feet and a light to my path." (Psalm 119:105)

"For what you have done I will always praise you in the presence of your faithful people. And I will hope in your name, for your name is good." (Psalm 52:9 NIV)

"Because your love is better than life, my lips will glorify you. I will praise you as long as I live, and in your name I will lift up my hands." (Psalm 63:3-4 NIV)

"How great are your works, Lord, how profound your thoughts!" (Psalm 92:5 NIV)

"You are my hiding place; You shall preserve me from trouble; You shall surround me with songs of deliverance." (Psalm 32:7)

"My lips will shout for joy when I sing praise to you because you have redeemed me." (Psalm 71:23 HCSB)

"I know that you can do anything, and no one can stop you." (Job 42:2 NLT)

"But I will sing of your strength, in the morning I will sing of your love; for you are my fortress, my refuge in times of trouble." (Psalm 59:16 NIV)

"How priceless is your unfailing love! Both high and low among men find refuge in the shadow of your wings." (Psalm 36:7)

5. PRACTICE WORSHIP PRAYERS

Have you ever tried to just say a prayer that was strictly 100% filled with praise and nothing else? Or strictly filled with thanksgiving? Or words of adoration? Or words of awe? Occasionally you should purposely do just that, and you will not only be practicing worship prayers, you will be worshiping as well! That is, if your prayer is heartfelt.

I remember going to a men's retreat years ago where the theme was prayer. There were many sermons and teachings on the different aspects of prayer. However, something was missing. There was not one sermon on prayers of praise. Yet, the Bible is filled with them.

At that retreat, there was a time set aside for public praying, where whoever wanted to could take turns praying out loud. People prayed for themselves, their family, their friends, for other people, and for many different situations. But there was not one prayer that was a worship prayer, for example, totally praise. So I tried it. Out loud. For the first time ever I just prayed 100% praise. And I liked it!

At first it was a little awkward. I wasn't used to it. I started out, "Father, I praise You." Then I went on just telling Him who He is – Lord, Master, Creator, etc. And then I proceeded to proclaim to Him many of His various titles, and all the things I could think of that He has the ability to do. I ended it with, "I give you all the honor and praise, and I pray this in the name of Jesus."

Don't get me wrong, I'm not saying we shouldn't pray for ourselves or others or anything else. We definitely should. But there is a time and place for every type of prayer.

I definitely learned something from my experience at that men's retreat. Because from then on, all my prayers would contain at least a portion of praise.

Even what is referred to as the Lord's prayer, the model prayer, contains praise.

"Our Father in heaven, Hallowed be Your name. Your kingdom come. Your will be done On earth as it is in heaven. Give us this day our daily bread. And forgive us our debts, As we forgive our debtors. And do not lead us into temptation, But deliver us from the evil one. For Yours is the kingdom and the power and the glory forever. Amen." **(Matthew 6:9-13)**

The above model prayer is like a prayer outline, taught by Jesus. Notice that the first sentence is praise, *"Our Father in heaven, Hallowed be Your name."* And the last sentence is also praise, *"For Yours is the kingdom and the power and the glory forever. Amen."*

Since the model prayer starts with praise, and ends with praise, at the very least that's how all our prayers should begin and end.

The model prayer is a great outline for us to use for general prayers. Worship prayers, however, are much more specific. Worship prayers are 100% thanksgiving, praise, adoration, or awe. Or a blend of them.

Try to practice worship prayers. Then you will be able to easily verbalize worship prayers over time, which means you will be able to respond to worship prompts more readily, and worship in the zone more freely.

Chapter 8

WORSHIP IN THE ZONE!

Does the concept of worship that has been presented in this book seem like a narrow view? That is precisely the way it should be! The broader the view of worship, the more diluted it becomes. A watered-down worship results in essentially no worship at all. If worship is everything, then it is nothing.

In true worship, we are giving God our complete attention. Our focus is totally on Him. Can you imagine how that must please God?

In this busy world, parents and children alike are very familiar with the term *quality time*. So many of the popular parenting books talk about making sure the limited time we spend with our children is quality time. Quality time is focused, purposeful, and meaningful. It's time specifically and totally devoted to each other.

Regarding worship, think of it as quality time with God. Worship is not doing our own thing without God, even if it is doing something that God may be pleased with.

Why did God create humans? The answer lies in a question that every sincere, responsible and loving parent could ask themselves, "Why do I want to have children?" God as Father created us that He may have a loving relationship with us as His loving children.

The more your relationship with the Lord grows, which is based in love, the more intimate and meaningful your worship becomes. Not only that, the easier it is to get in the zone with Him.

When you are worshiping in the zone, it's that special moment when time stands still and your total focus is on the Lord. It's when you deliberately come before Him, and express heartfelt thanksgiving, praise, adoration, or awe to God. And it can happen anywhere and at anytime. It's when you sincerely and gratefully acknowledge who He is and what He does. Worship is a spiritual encounter with God.

The act of worship is always a one way street – from you to God. It has nothing to do with you. It's all about Him. It's never a time when you are asking or praying for something for yourself. It's a time of complete focus on Him alone. When this special moment of worship occurs, you are in the zone with God, and you know it!

Don't let your concept of worship be one that is watered-down and meaningless. Grow in your worship and let it drive you to live for Him. Worship Him often and it will refresh your motivation and your intimacy. Make your worship a rich experience and a joy.

Remember that the Father is seeking true worshipers – those who worship in spirit and in truth. May you grow in knowledge and grace of Him who seeks those types of people, and may you be the worshiper he seeks.

Isn't it amazing that our worship is just a preview of the worship that we will be participating in when we enter heaven? Even more amazing is the fact that heaven's worship is going on right now, waiting for us to join in. What a great day that will be!

In the meantime, as long as it is called today, worship the Lord your God!

APPENDIX A: WORSHIP EXAMPLES

(A SAMPLING OF BIBLE WORSHIP SCENES)

There are dozens of worship scenes in the Bible. By looking at them, you can get a good concept of what worship looks like. Below is just a sampling of the many such scenes.

JESUS WALKS ON WATER

One of my favorite worship moments in the Bible that exemplifies worship in the zone occurs in a boat. This particular miracle and subsequent worship of Jesus is recorded in Matthew chapter 14. It's the episode of Jesus miraculously walking on water. Jesus had sent the disciples in a boat to cross the lake while he went up on a mountain to pray. The disciples didn't do so well because of the strong wind. Jesus had stayed on the mountain alone most of the night because He wanted to do what He seemed to cherish – pray in solitude.

Toward the early morning hours, He came to them, walking on the water, in the wind. The disciples cried out in fear thinking Jesus was a ghost. He responded, "Take courage! It is I. Don't be afraid." Then Peter responded, "Lord, if it's you, tell me to come to you on the water." Jesus said, "Come". So Peter jumped out of the boat and walked on the water too – for a short while. As soon as he saw the wind, and the waves, and realized he could die out there, he cried for help.

Jesus came to his rescue, both of them climbing into the boat. The wind died down and that's the moment the disciples worshiped Jesus – right there in the boat, right in front of Him. The original Greek word for worship that is used in that verse means to bow down.

Can you imagine? I'm sure after seeing the impossible, the disciples literally bowed, or even fell down, at the feet of Jesus. Matthew 14:33 states that the disciples exclaimed, *"Truly you are the Son of God."* This is a great example of true worship.

I love this worship scene because it clearly exhibits the three keys to worship. First, the disciples certainly had an encounter with Jesus. Secondly, they no doubt had sincere, heartfelt attitudes. And thirdly, they expressed their worship when they fell down at Jesus' feet, and said "Truly you are the Son of God."

JESUS APPEARS AFTER THE RESURRECTION

Mary Magdalene and the other Mary had come to the tomb early on the Sunday morning after Jesus died. Incredible things happened there. An angel rolled back the stone that sealed off the entrance to the tomb. The guards who witnessed it were so afraid they shook and fell like dead men. Then the women listened in amazement as the angel spoke directly to them. He told them that Jesus had risen from the dead, that they should go look in the tomb for themselves and then go tell the disciples.

As the women hurried away from the tomb, the Bible says they were afraid yet filled with joy. In other words, they were experiencing all kinds of emotion: excitement, fear, wonder, awe, thrill, exhilaration, anticipation, elation, jubilation, to name a few. However, that was just the beginning.

On their way to tell the others the great news, they were intercepted - stopped in their tracks. They encountered Jesus. What happened next gives us a great visual. The women fell down before Him, embraced His feet and worshiped Him.

"So they went out quickly from the tomb with fear and great joy, and ran to bring His disciples word. And as they went to tell His disciples, behold, Jesus met them, saying, 'Rejoice!' So they came and held Him by the feet and worshiped Him." (Matthew 28:8-9)

This is another great worship scene that clearly exhibits the three keys to real worship. They encountered Jesus, certainly had heartfelt attitudes, and bowed before Him embracing His feet.

JESUS CURES A BLIND MAN

In John chapter 9, worship is shown to us by the blind man who was given sight by Jesus. This man was born blind. Jesus put mud on his eyes and told him to go wash in the pool of Siloam. When he did just that, the impossible happened. He miraculously was given something he never experienced before – sight.

Many who witnessed the event were doubtful and inquisitive. First, they accused the man of being someone different from the blind man whom they always had seen begging, saying that he just looked like the blind man. Then they questioned the identity of Jesus Himself. In addition to all that, the Pharisees were upset because all this happened on a Sabbath day. Jesus caused a stir and the man born blind was questioned about Jesus.

Because of his blindness, he obviously could not see the face of the one who performed the miracle, but only knew that His name was Jesus. Sometime later, he again encountered Jesus.

"Jesus heard that they had cast him out; and when He had found him, He said to him, 'Do you believe in the Son of God?' He answered and said, 'Who is He, Lord, that I may believe in Him?' And Jesus said to him, 'You have both seen Him and it is He who is talking with you.' Then he said, 'Lord, I believe!' And he worshiped Him." (John 9:35-38)

Once again we see worship happening in this scene. The man encounters Jesus with an obvious heartfelt attitude, and expresses worship, "Lord, I believe."

There are so many other great worship scenes in the Bible. Reviewing them gives us more insight on what real worship looks like. Below is just a sampling. Some are very simple, but very powerful.

THE ISRAELITES WORSHIP

"Then Moses and Aaron went and gathered together all the elders of the children of Israel. And Aaron spoke all the words which the Lord had spoken to Moses. Then he did the signs in the sight of the people. So the people believed; and when they heard that the Lord had visited the children of Israel and that He had looked on their affliction, then they bowed their heads and worshiped." (Exodus 4:29-31)

KING HEZEKIAH AND THE PEOPLE WORSHIP

"So all the assembly worshiped, the singers sang, and the trumpeters sounded; all this continued until the burnt offering was finished. And when they had finished offering, the king and all who were present with him bowed and worshiped. Moreover King Hezekiah and the leaders commanded the Levites to sing praise to the Lord with the words of David and of Asaph the seer. So they sang praises with gladness, and they bowed their heads and worshiped." (2 Chronicles 29:28-30)

EZRA LEADS THE PEOPLE IN WORSHIP

"And Ezra blessed the Lord, the great God. Then all the people answered, 'Amen, Amen!' while lifting up their hands. And they bowed their heads and worshiped the Lord with their faces to the ground." (Nehemiah 8:6)

THE DISCIPLES WORSHIP JESUS

"And He led them out as far as Bethany, and He lifted up His hands and blessed them. Now it came to pass, while He blessed them, that He was parted from them and carried up into heaven. And they worshiped Him, and returned to Jerusalem with great joy." (Luke 24:50-52)

JEHOSHAPHAT AND THE PEOPLE WORSHIP

"And Jehoshaphat bowed his head with his face to the ground, and all Judah and the inhabitants of Jerusalem bowed before the Lord, worshiping the Lord." **(Chronicles 20:18)**

JOB WORSHIPS

"Then Job arose, tore his robe, and shaved his head; and he fell to the ground and worshiped." **(Job 1:20)**

JACOB WORSHIPS

"By faith Jacob, when he was dying, blessed each of Joseph's sons, and worshiped as he leaned on the top of his staff." **(Hebrews 11:21)**

APPENDIX B: MY PERSONAL JOURNEY

(From Volunteer to Full-Time Worship Leader)

In 1986, my wife and I realized we needed to get more serious in our spiritual walk, so we joined a Bible based church group of about 15 people that was meeting in a house. We hadn't gone to church in a long time.

A few months after joining, the small church building they had already started to build was completed, so we began meeting there. The services were very traditional, very conservative – old hymns, most written in the 1800's, led by a piano and anyone who could at least try to sing.

Someone found out I was a musician, so they convinced me to at least play along with the piano. I tried. And I did, sort of reluctantly. Playing old hymns in 3/4 time was not what I preferred. But I played along. I must admit, some of the hymns were fun to play.

I'm not against hymns, don't get me wrong, many of the hymns are certainly great, and are timeless. It's just that as a musician, I was used to playing a more contemporary style of music on my acoustic guitar. If you are a musician, you know what I mean.

Of course, in 1986, there weren't a lot of contemporary Christian bands like there are today. The worship movement, musically, was in its infancy. As the contemporary Christian genre grew, I grew along with it. I kind of rode the wave.

I always listened to music, and tried to stay relevant. That attitude still helps me today. We are certainly blessed to have so much Christian music today. The internet has opened up an entire realm of music accessibility. It's fantastic.

Back to the small church. I was playing guitar along with the piano. Then they found out I could sing too. Actually, I do not consider myself a very good singer. But they convinced me to sing once in a while. It was at this time that I began to write some Christian songs.

The slow, grueling transition from ancient hymns to a more contemporary style of music really began when our original preacher left, and a new, young preacher was hired. He was a visionary. And he wanted to take our church of about 40 people in a new direction.

So things started to change, and I was all for it. And yes, it was slow and grueling. The original piano player was the first preacher's wife, and when he left, she obviously left with him. There were a couple of piano players in the congregation, so one of them stepped up to play. Like the first pianist, they played out of the hymn book, sight reading the sheet music. On the other hand, I played by ear. I couldn't sight read.

Now let me tell you a little bit about the conflict that I felt back then about the piano player reading music and me playing by ear. One was technical and the other feel. One was mechanical and the other emotional. One was locked in, the other spontaneous. One was unwavering, the other improvisational.

Remember, my background was playing in bands, with other musicians. Playing along with the piano was not a good fit for me.

When you think about it, the piano was basically meant to be a solo instrument in a church setting. The right hand covered the melody. The left hand covered the bass notes and the rhythm of the song. You sang along with the melody of the piano.

I was coming more from a band perspective. In a band, you didn't need a piano playing the melody because you sang the melody. You didn't need the piano playing the bass notes because you had a bass guitar. You didn't need the piano playing rhythm because you had a drummer. The piano then, in a band setting, was to be used and played differently, to embellish what was going on musically.

The piano therefore would be one of the hardest obstacles to overcome in the process of transforming our church from a very traditional hymn based service to a contemporary Christian style.

Eventually, I was asked to lead some songs with my acoustic guitar. That posed another challenge for me. Early on I would describe our music as being piano driven as opposed to guitar driven. In other words, the piano was the lead instrument, starting the songs, and ending the songs. My acoustic guitar was basically just an accompaniment to the piano. If I were to lead, the guitar would need to be the lead instrument. That's a total 180.

The songs and music, therefore, needed to become guitar driven instead of piano driven. The piano needed to follow me, instead of me following the piano. Can you see the conflict? This was new for the piano player who was sight reading. And even more of a challenge for the piano player who was trying to play a contemporary song instead of a hymn.

I would eventually take away another "ministry" – the sight reading piano player. It was unfortunate, but in the big picture of things, it needed to happen.

I tried to coach the piano player to learn chords instead of playing the melody. I was singing the melody, so we didn't need to hear that on the piano. I started to write out chords. However, the piano player at the time just couldn't get the feel of playing differently, and without sheet music. So another piano player jumped in, and actually did well with the transition to chords.

This experience led me to my rule that I use today – if you need to read music, you can't be in the band! I was looking for musicians who could play together with feel, with the ability to listen and react to each other, to express themselves musically within the realm of the song we were playing. That's what I grew up doing, and that's what I wanted in the church.

Eventually, I took the role of being the guitar playing "song leader". I felt if I were to lead a song, I needed to like the song – to connect with that song. Otherwise, I was just singing and playing superficially. This led to another challenge. If I were to start leading all songs, I needed to start picking the songs myself. I suppose I took away several "ministries" as we transitioned from traditional to contemporary music. This time it was selecting the songs for Sunday mornings.

Since I starting playing music in the church, I continually prayed that the Lord would provide musicians. I always envisioned a band. After all, that was my background and my passion – to play with other musicians.

Well, the Lord didn't let me down. An electric guitarist came into the congregation – the same incredible guitarist who is still with me today. Eventually, other musicians came – a bass player, and later a drummer.

We continued to grow musically, and the congregation also grew and grew. Personally, I not only grew musically, I grew spiritually. I mean I dug into the Bible with intensity. I studied and eventually began teaching Bible studies. My relationship with the Lord grew closer and closer. Not only was I leading music, but I became a member of the leadership in the church, part of the team making spiritual decisions and future direction decisions for the congregation.

As I matured spiritually, I began writing more songs. I'm still writing. For me, if I am still writing songs, I feel it's a reflection of my spiritual condition and growth. And that's a good thing. I'm thankful for it.

Over time, our congregation grew from one service to two. Then from two services to three. We made major, but gradual changes to the church building. Every change was another step in bringing us from a very traditional church to a very contemporary church.

But it took years and years. Slowly, the building itself transformed. At one point we took the pews out and replaced them with chairs. Later on we took down the old style chandeliers and replaced them with receded ceiling lights. At one point we moved the stage from the back of the auditorium to the side, and fanned all the chairs in a semi-circle around it. It was an idea the teens used on a youth night, and we took their creativity and adopted it for Sunday mornings. A short time later we decided to use controlled lighting, so we actually boarded up the windows!

The windows were situated so that anyone seated inside could look outside. What's worse is that the sidewalk leading to the church building ran right next to the windows, so anyone arriving late walked the length of the building, in sight of everyone. Even worse than this, the building was located on a four lane highway, and if someone was pulled over for speeding, that drew more attention than the sermon.

So, we boarded up the windows, and painted the plywood the same color as the walls. That stopped that problem. It laid the foundation for me to be always conscious of the issue of distraction in a worship service.

A short time later, we added stage lights and dimmers so that we could change the mood in the building, since there was now no outside lighting entering the building.

My theory was that we had only 15 to 20 minutes to take a congregation from their crazy world on the outside to a point of worship and focus on the inside, in preparation to hear the sermon. That's not an easy task. So I needed every tool to do that – controlled lighting and a conscious effort to reduce any other distractions.

The controlled lighting wasn't as effective with a white ceiling – a hold over from the old days. So we painted the ceiling a dark, dark blue – almost black. That worked great.

By this time, the congregation was conditioned for change. This would be a great benefit for future change and creativity. It also convinced me that to have an effective worship service, it wasn't so much about trying to make each Sunday better, but it was more important to change things up. That way, the services never became stale, but were fresh and somewhat different. This still applies today.

We would switch the service around from week to week. Sometimes moving the sermon closer to the front or more toward the end of the service. Sometimes we would do the Lord's Supper earlier in the service, sometimes last.

Eventually, we outgrew our original building, and moved into a brand new campus. All the concepts we had learned we applied to the design of the new building – the controlled lighting, the floor plan, and the philosophy of minimal distractions.

All the while the Lord kept adding musicians and singers, and even other song writers. My desire to have a very talented band became a reality. I attribute it all to God's hand, not mine.

I began a songwriting club. It was called "The 33:3 Club". It was based on Psalm 33:3 which says, "Sing a new song, play skillfully, and shout for joy." We had about 10 songwriters, the youngest was 12 years old.

I would give them a scripture passage, and we all had to write a song based on it. At first I gave everyone two weeks, but later lighted up a bit on the deadline.

When everyone was finished, we had a special church service on a Sunday night or Wednesday night where everyone played their song.

From my first days of writing and playing music in our church, using an occasional original song became somewhat of a given in our services. The same holds true today.

Early on, I didn't think about being a worship leader. I don't remember that title even existing back then. I was just a musician trying to express myself, leading others to sing songs. I guess you could say I was a song leader.

I understood song leading, but I didn't grasp the concept of worship leading at first. I have come to realize that almost anyone who can sing can be a song leader in front of a congregation, but there is a big difference between a song leader and a worship leader. The key to being an effective worship leader is this – you need to be a worshiper first! And to be a worshiper you must understand what worship is. This came in due time.

I faithfully played music, wrote songs, and led other musicians, as well as the congregation, all as a volunteer. I did this for nearly 17 years, before becoming a full-time Worship Leader. During that time, the role of a worship leader in a contemporary Christian church began to be recognized as an important ministry position.

As our church grew, there was a need for more staff. The next logical move was to add me as a paid minister, so I could devote my efforts full-time, and not just on a volunteer basis.

The question was, "When?" I was working as a quality manager for a manufacturing factory making very good money. How could I just quit and take a major pay cut to enter full time ministry, raising a family of five as the sole breadwinner? I prayed for God to open a door for me to see when the timing was right.

In January of 2003, we scheduled our usual leadership retreat. Once a year, the leadership team of our church would meet in a borrowed oceanfront condo for an all-night brainstorming session, casting a vision for the upcoming year. We were to meet on a Friday night.

A few days prior to the leadership retreat, the preacher told me confidentially that at some point during our overnighter, he wanted to bring up the possibility of me being the next paid staff member. He just wanted to make sure there was a unanimous approval for my appointment, even though we weren't certain of when that would happen.

I was at work on that Friday afternoon, in my office, thinking about the upcoming church leadership retreat. The phone on my desk rang. It was someone from Human Resources. They asked me to come to the office.

I sat across from the H.R. Director with the door closed. She then proceeded to bluntly tell me that there was a big company downsizing. About 125 people were being let go, and I was one of them! She said that my termination was not caused by my performance, but simply that the company was in financial trouble and needed to cut employees.

I was speechless. I'm sure my eyes were huge and my mouth was open in a state of shock. She must have thought that I was taking it really hard. In reality, I wasn't in shock about losing my job, I was in total amazement of God's perfect timing!

I had been praying hard for God to open a door and let me know the right time to quit my job and go into full time ministry. He answered the prayer right then and there without a doubt. It was like He not only opened a door, but opened a hanger door and drop kicked me right through it! It was like God was saying, "What are you waiting for?"

I was so excited to see God at work, that right in that room, I began telling the H.R. Director about the Lord's answered prayer. She may have thought I was crazy, but I didn't care.

Things happened fast. They told me to pack up my desk right away, box everything up, and I was free to go that very afternoon. In other words, they sort of wanted me to leave right away.

As I was emptying my desk and packing up my things, I called my wife. I said, "You won't believe this, but I just lost my job!" Knowing my desire to go into music ministry full time, she said, "That's the best thing that ever happened!"

I hung up and called my preacher next. Again I said, "You won't believe this, but I just lost my job!" He said, "I think God is trying to tell us something!"

Then he told me he was going to still bring up the discussion of me being the next full time, paid minister. However, he didn't want me to say anything about losing my job until he disclosed it. He didn't want my approval to be based on the fact the I lost my job. So that night, I waited and waited and waited. We started about 6 p.m. By

83

10 p.m., he still didn't bring up the discussion on my possible future position. I was going insane with anticipation, thinking about that afternoon, losing my job, my family, and my future direction that I wanted to take.

I was so absolutely convinced that God opened the door to ministry for me, that I decided in no way would I look for another job. I would trust that God would provide for me, and believed that He wanted me serving the Kingdom full time. Therefore, I anxiously awaited our discussion.

Finally, around 11 p.m., the preacher brought up the possibility of me coming on full time. He asked if anyone had any objections. No one did. Just the opposite. Everyone unanimously was for me, and encouraged me.

Then he dropped the bombshell and told everyone what happened to me that afternoon, revealing God's hand moving, and His perfect timing being executed.

It was quite overwhelming. Everyone was amazed and praised God. One of the leaders later told me that it was one of the most spiritual experiences of his life!

So, I went into full time ministry, feeling that it was God's plan to put me there. During the next few days I received calls, emails, and cards congratulating me on losing my job. Someone even baked me a cake to celebrate. I never imagined so many people being happy about someone losing their job.

The Lord provided for us in ways beyond what I could ever have imagined. On paper, there was no way we could make it financially, but somehow it all worked out. We tithed faithfully, and God kept His promise to bless us abundantly. And He continues to do so to this very day.

To Him be the glory forever, Amen!

ABOUT THE AUTHOR

Chip Vickio grew up in Watkins Glen, N.Y., and moved near Rehoboth Beach, Delaware, in 1978 with his wife, Francie. They have been there ever since. They have three children.

Chip has been involved in worship leading for more than 25 years in a contemporary Christian church.

He is a Christ Follower, Worship Leader, Musician, Singer, Song Writer, Author, Blogger, and Bible Teacher.

Made in the USA
Las Vegas, NV
21 December 2024

15152633R00056